HE Remembered me...

Dianne M. Towns

HE Remembered me
ISBN: 9781974372553
(C)Copyright 2017

Unless otherwise identified, "Scripture quotations taken from the Amplified Bible (AMP) Copyright (c) 2015 by The Lockman Foundation Used by permission www.Lockman.org

Dedication

This book is dedicated to You, Lord. Thank you Jesus for your faithfulness to me and to all the men and women of this world who are yet holding on to their faith, because "we" know that faith is what it takes to please Him! I stand with you, believe with you and hope with you that the Supernatural grace of God is sufficient for you as you wait.

God is no respecter of persons. He made a promise to me and He kept it. Your manifestation awaits. Do not be discouraged, I believe it is reaping season!

Gal. 6:9

Let us not grow weary or become discouraged in doing good, for at the proper time we will reap, if we do not give in.

Contents

Acknowledgments

Thanks to all of my extended family members at Fresh Anointing House of Worship.

Thank you, Calvin and Tammy for lending me your ideas. God Bless.

Thank you "Ant" Hill for your "red pen".

Mrs. Howard, words cannot express my gratitude for our friendship and your matchless generosity.

Bishop Kyle and Pastor Kemi Searcy, thank you for your relentless display of Christ.

"Pastor Jeff"…you were right about His grace. Thank you!

Jannai and Marilyn, in my weakness, through your prayers I was made strong. Thank you both.

To my three beautiful ladies, Briana, Celina and Jasmyne; there is nothing too hard for God! Carry that with you always.

Foreword

Far too many believers live our lives, fight our battles, and exercise our faith without tapping into the incredible grace which God has provided for us.

When I speak of grace, I am not referencing the grace or unmerited favour that we all encountered at our moment of salvation but that which is called enabling grace. It is a grace which gives you an inner strength and resolve which spawns an undeniable faith to empower you to keep on going; to keep on believing; to keep on fighting until you see the results of that which you have trusted the Lord for.

He Remembered Me is a wonderful true account of how one woman tapped into this reservoir of grace and was able to continue to love a man when her love for him was totally rejected by him. It gave her hope to continue to believe "the word of the Lord" and experience the "inner death" that kept her praying for a husband's destiny, as he walked away from their marriage.

After reading this book you will be challenged to tap into this Amazing Grace, and then like Dianne, you will truly know that God will not put more on you than you can bear.

Troy Towns

Introduction

I was going through a very tough trial in my life, yet the Lord impressed upon my heart to journal that trial and many of the dreams He gave me along with it. That journal became the inspiration for my first book.

As I wrote *I Remember Joseph*, I did not know how to put things into words at first. All I knew was that God had made a promise to me. Although nothing in my life remotely resembled His promise I decided to "try God". I must admit though, that there were periods of time when doubt crept into my mind...I kept saying to myself, but it hasn't happened. How can I write a book about these things and tell others what I believe God is doing while yet believing for God to do it?

I did not have a rebuttal for that doubt and for a season I put the idea to rest and walked by sight. Things were really bad and at times the impossible was more vivid than the hope of His glory. Yet, I could not help but recall *2 Corinthians. 5:7...*

for we walk by faith, not by sight.

Until this time in my life, I honestly thought I had faith. No, I thought I had TALL faith, until one setback after another challenged me in every way imaginable. But, there was one thing calling me to stand. God cannot lie!

Man can and will lie. Man will and he does lie! Man seems to lie better than he tells the truth. The example I had before me was that of betrayal, deception and instability and if God was anything like man, surely He would not keep His promise either. But, what if He really is real and what if He really cannot lie, then I might be missing out on something.

Well there was only one way to find out. I would have to trust Him. But, trusting had always led to disappointment and heartache, so how could I break free of my self-protective stance and relinquish my heart to *possibly* obtain something that was *merely* a promise I believed to have come from God? What if I trust? What if I believe? What if nothing changes and I find myself let down once again? Could I bear it? Well, since He will not allow me to be tempted beyond what I can bear, then sure I can bear it.

1 Corinthians 10:13

but God is faithful, who will not suffer you to be tempted above that ye are able

Deuteronomy 31:6 tells me He will never leave nor forsake me, therefore I can and I will trust Him. Since He cannot lie, then surely I can take Him at His word. And since His word says, "Without faith it is impossible to please and be satisfactory to Him", I had my work cut out for me.

Hebrews 11:6
Without faith it is impossible to please God.

I wanted so desperately to please Him. Nothing was more important to me than the pursuit of pleasing the Master.

I began to envision the domino effect. I said out loud to the Lord one day, "Lord, if You really do this, how many marriages will be restored?" I was literally in awe of the possibility that others would hear my story and be encouraged to stand. I saw women standing therefore, having done all to stand! I saw men, standing therefore, having done all to stand! I could picture the thousands of couples on the verge of divorce, yet there would be one opting to walk in forgiveness choosing longsuffering over surrender because he/she read my story. I saw many things in my mind and began to praise God for the vivid picture, but the ultimate question still remained. CAN YOU GO FIRST?

Will you endure to the end without fainting? What if things take a turn for the worse? Will you continue to profess His word? Will you continue no matter what? The answer to these questions had to be yes. It was not just about me. It became about everyone out there who needed something to hope for. Somebody out there needs to see that someone stood in the midst of adversity and the God of today, showed up and revealed yet again that He's still in the blessing business. Excuse the cliché, but somebody reading this needed to hear that.

I love the Lord, and I love reading His word. The stories about David and Job are phenomenal and I can't get enough of the memories of my friend Joseph, but I wanted to see God do something now. I wanted to know that the God I serve and encourage others to serve really does have a perspective that surpasses all comprehension and His word still works today.

How can a gentle answer turn away wrath? When wrath comes are we not accustomed to defending ourselves? I sure was. Of course I was. Now what?

Proverbs 15:1
A soft answer turns away wrath, but grievous words stir up anger.

How can you say something is what it does not appear to be and it become so?

Romans 4:17
call those things which be not as though they were...

If my husband does not obey the word of God, shouldn't I point it out to him and help him to see the error of his ways? What is this stuff about being in subjection to him so that even if he does not obey the word, I can have a direct affect on him by the way I conduct myself?

1 Peter 3:1

In like manner, you married women, be submissive to your own husbands [subordinate yourselves as being secondary to and dependent on them, and adapt yourselves to them], so that even if any do not obey the Word [of God], they may be won over not by discussion but by the [godly] lives of their wives,

2 When they observe the pure and modest way in which you conduct yourselves, together with your reverence [for your husband; you are to feel for him all that reverence includes: to respect, defer to, revere him—to honour, esteem, appreciate, prize, and, in the human sense, to adore him, that is, to admire, praise, be devoted to, deeply love, and enjoy your husband].

3 Let not yours be the [merely] external adorning with [elaborate] interweaving and knotting of the hair, the wearing of jewelry, or changes of clothes;

4 But let it be the inward adorning and beauty of the hidden person of the heart, with the incorruptible and unfading charm of a gentle and peaceful spirit, which [is not anxious or wrought up, but] is very precious in the sight of God.

Is this foolishness or fact? Is this truth or fiction? Is this fantasy or faith? Well, there was only one way to find out and yes, I would have to go, not only first, but all the way... and so let us begin again with this one...

I ended my book, *I Remember Joseph* on a high note of encouragement to all those who are on this faith journey, with the following:

Somewhere along the way, God picked my fight with Satan, and He said, "What about my servant, Dianne?" He identified me by name knowing that I could and would bear this burden for the sake of His glory and for all those who needed to glean from His fulfilled promise to me. If that is you, then know this... You are "the called" and *He* called *you* by name, just as He did me...

He said, this one I've been preparing since birth...

This one is not by accident! This one is not by happenstance!

But, this one is "the called" according to My purpose!

I have a purpose for her that no other woman can fulfil... that no other woman can bear... that no other woman is willing to endure...

This one I have called specifically for this time and for this purpose...

This one has let patience have her perfect work in her...

This one has used gentle answers to turn away wrath...

This one has prayed the effectual fervent prayers...

This one has worn the breastplate of my righteousness...

This one sought after peace and pursued it...

This one remained steadfast and unmovable...

This one called those things that be not as though they were...

This one remembered My word and that I watch after it to perform it...

This one committed her ways unto the Lord...

This one spoke to the mountains with faith...

This one fasted and prayed...

This one remembered the weapons of our warfare are not carnal... This one knew her weapons were mighty through God to the pulling down of strongholds...

This one walked by faith and not by sight...

This one had confidence in Me that I heard her petition that lined up with My will...

This one kept Me in remembrance of My word...

This one remembered I Am not a man... I cannot lie

This one remembered I must keep My promise...

This one knew I would not deny Myself the glory of fulfilling her promise...

This one made it about Me...

This one was struck down, but not destroyed...

This one, having done all to stand...is standing therefore!!!

This one understands My divine perspective!

This one remembered Joseph and the fulfilment of the promise made to him...

This one knows that I Am no respecter of persons.

This one knows that what I did for Joseph...

With all that said, I submit to you now that *He remembered me*!

Chapter 1

A Look Back

The Lord continued to endow me with grace upon grace as I stood and believed. I ended my final chapter of *I Remember Joseph* with the divine perspective that although I am in this and I have yet to see the manifestation of the promise, this is where I have to remain in my thoughts that I may obtain the prize in due season.

At times I still wondered; will I be able to keep this up? Can I truly endure and continue to hope beyond what I see before me? What if it does not happen? I could have moved on and this could be far behind me right now. Thoughts came to mind like, what if you misinterpreted the dreams? Are dreams really of God? Am I just seeing what I want to see, etcetera?

Each time one of those thoughts came to mind, I just could not hold back what was inside me..., "But God!"

There has always been a stubbornness and a determination inside me since I was a small, unsaved, unsanctified and un-Holy Ghost filled young girl...things just had to make sense to me and they still do! So in these times, that stubbornness would kick in and I would ask myself, the following questions:

What am I certain of?

Okay, God is real!

What do I know about Him?

He cannot lie!

What proof do I have that He will do what He says?

Well, besides some testimonies over the years and some manifestations of things I have witnessed in other people's lives and in many bible stories, I had not seen any real, right now, God-is-speaking-to-me-and-He's-going-to-reveal-it-to-me, situations.

I came to rely on the story of Joseph, but I also wanted to see for myself that yes, beyond the norm and beyond the daily provisions and occasional healings and manifestations and the obvious (He woke me up this morning) blessing, that there was absolute proof of God's existence and His blessing.

So then, if this was really Him speaking to me and showing me these things, I would have to do what He said and not what I was thinking...what He said and not what I wanted...what He said in spite of my feelings, etcetera. I had yet to do either of these things, so now I must BELIEVE! UNTIL I RECEIVE! That was the only option.

I had been saying that I believed God, and I really believed that I did, but where were my blessings from this God in Whom I believed? Hmmm...So, I had to brace myself and my faith; lace up my shoes of perseverance and walk this thing out! Once again, I was back on the road to a promise fulfilled, but things didn't just turn around like magic. I did see evidence that God was at work in my life and prophetic utterances were coming true right in front of me, but still this man (my husband) had not come full circle back into my life. But, let me say this...

I was desperate to see that God is real! I was desperate to know that He truly is a rewarder of those who diligently seek Him.

Hebrews 11:6
he is a rewarder of them that diligently seek him.

I know that man will lie to me. I even expect it. I know to not put my trust in man, but in God. Yet, this God had not made good on His promise, so something was still hanging in the balance.

Almost as if the little girl in me had taken over, I was bent on getting my answers. Man could not just tell me any old thing and expect me to believe it. Things had to add up and make sense and at least seem real or possible. I did not know why I was that way, but evidently it was something the Lord put in me at a very young age to prepare me for what was happening now. I wasn't stubborn for just no real reason. As a God fearing adult woman now, I had a destiny and a calling on my life that would require that stubbornness in the midst of a trial. That stubbornness was the key to my now, unwavering faith in Him and His ability to truly do ALL things!

I realized the burden of proof wasn't on my shoulders but rested on the integrity of the All Mighty God! God if you truly are real and You cannot lie, then you must do this (because You said You would) and I'm just stubborn enough to watch and wait! So, that's just what I did...

As I watched and waited, He began to speak clearly. God gave me dreams, He would have to cause them to come to pass. He spoke words over me; He would have to cause them to come to pass. He gave me grace and hope for the impossible; He would have to prove that He would not allow me to be put to shame.

There was a relentless desperation in me that said, God I have to know You will not fail me. If You fail me, there is nothing else left. There is no God. There is no Christianity. There is no faith. There is no hope, and there are no dreams! That is where I was. God would have to keep His promise to me. But in order for Him to do that, I would have to continue to have faith and believe; walk uprightly and continue to confess His word in the midst of pain, fear, frustration, doubt (at times) and anger. I would have to endure a few more bumps and bruises and bandage a few more wounds. Could I do it? Could I go yet another day? Could I look past my scars and hold back my tears in order that God could truly be glorified? If not for His grace, that answer would be No! But, His grace truly is sufficient...

Many times we grow weary and faint before we obtain the promise of God. We accept defeat and kiss our promise goodbye and begin to make our acceptance speech. Have you ever said, Well, I did all I could but nothing happened. Or, I stood on the promise but God will not violate a person's will so I just choose to let it go and move on?

So have I and just before the manifestation of my promise I briefly revisited that thought. But then I saw your face. You, reading this book right now...I saw you lose hope and I saw you picking up the towel, but please before you throw it in, read on...

Chapter 2
It has to be about Him...

Hebrews 11:6

*But without faith it is impossible to please and be satisfactory to Him. For whoever would come near to God must [necessarily] believe that God exists and that He **is** the rewarder of those who earnestly and diligently seek Him [out].*

My walk had been a walk of faith, without which it is impossible to please God. I had always taken pride in the fact that I simply wanted to please God even if my husband never changed. I wanted to be obedient to the point where I was a vessel being used by God for His purpose only. It did not matter that my flesh hurt, worried, wondered or even wanted to have some pleasure of its own; what mattered was that God would be glorified by the outcome of my obedience which would yield the fruit that others would see and strive for. What mattered was that my sacrifice would promote hope and faith amongst believers to stand therefore and begin to re-establish what a covenant really means.

A covenant is a contract or agreement. When two people marry, they enter into a contract with one another and with God indicating that what God has joined together no man can put it asunder (it has to be about Him). We are united until death do us part. Please do not confuse this with the world's legal contract based on the theory of if..., then...

Although my husband chose to violate this covenant and yes, I did have a justifiable way out of my marriage based on his infidelity, I know the Lord continued to impress upon my heart that His perfect will would do more for the Kingdom of Light than my permissive will would do for my flesh.

Christ did not deserve the cross but He endured it for my sake and yours. Could I not endure for a season of time that He might be glorified? Of course I could but only by His grace! The Lord continued to give me grace for every setback.

My husband and I were separated for several months off and on prior to finally divorcing. During these months of separation he would come to visit the children quite frequently. Each time the Lord would give me grace.

I must admit that I allowed my flesh to dictate my actions at times and I would try to rearrange my schedule just so I could be home when he came by (I made it about me). I kept thinking that he would eventually see what he was missing or giving up on, so it motivated me to keep my appearance up. I dressed well, kept my hair done, and always had my make-up on. I thought, maybe I don't have the privilege of his affection but I would at least be pleasing to his eye.

Ladies, no matter what any person says about you, know who God says you are and walk uprightly, with your head held high (make it about Him). If your husband is saying derogatory things to you, you don't have to agree with him. When you agree with it that is what empowers the enemy using him to get the best of you. Do not allow anyone to speak anything over you that you have the power to change or correct. If nothing else, find out what the Lord has to say about it and walk in it until you see it in you, on you, and through you!

As I said, I did everything I could to be attractive for my husband. Sometimes he took notice and sometimes he seemed to ignore me. But in those moments when he did not ignore me I was thinking to myself, *as much as he loathed the idea of being my husband, what is this look for? Why is he flirting with me? If I were really as mean and sorry and worthless as he said, then why would he have any interest in me whatsoever?* There it was again…this does not make sense, so yes there had to be an explanation. Anytime something does not make sense to me, I seek out an explanation and just as the bible says, I always find what I am looking for.

Though the rejection was still gripping, I praised God for every smirk, every smile, every kind word, every good deed and every opportunity to pray.

The more I prayed, the more I began to change on the inside and while I still kept up with the things on the outside, the glow was coming from within. I knew the Lord was still moulding me and shaping me and I began to fashion myself after His heart and not my own. I made it about Him!

While at first, I wanted to look good for my husband, the Lord shifted my focus onto Him. I began to desire holiness and humility along with grace, patience and peace. I wanted God to look upon me and not have to turn His face from me because of sin, whether it was in thought or deed. So, I asked the Lord to show me where there was still error in my life or in my heart.

He then revealed to me that I was focusing too much still on getting the man's attention, although He did not caution me to change my dress. He did, however, begin to stifle the anxieties and the anticipations in me and yet awaken a new desire in me to be chaste. I still kept up my appearance, but I was not trying to flaunt it in front of my husband, I just simply enjoyed the newness, and the elegance and the presence of God that was in me in such a way that my attire was not on me, but it was me. I was beautiful, for the first time in my life, and I knew it.

As the Lord lifted my countenance and allowed me to see that I was simply beautiful in His sight, I did not care whether my husband saw it, I just knew that he could not miss it and it was a blessing to him if he just happened to capture a glimpse of me, simply due to the light and the glory upon me which he was so desperately lacking.

Sometimes, I would even get dressed up and go out of the house when I knew he was on the way, because even though he was my husband and I had desired his approval, the spirit of manipulation is still witchcraft! Whether it is a wife wooing a wayward husband or vice versa, the motive has to be a godly one and not a self-seeking one. My motives initially, were just that, self-seeking. I wanted results and I had been allowing the enemy to use me to try to make my husband see or feel or realize a thing, but only God can put His glory on you. The Lord would send me out of the house until I understood this.

As I let Him have His way in me, He was then allowing the Holy Spirit to minister to my husband. He began to miss me. He began to have a different type of longing for me. Not because of me, or what I was wearing, but because of Who I was yielding to and who I was becoming. I don't care what you put on, if you're only appealing to the lust in a man, you're not making any real progress. For me, it was time to be that good thing! It was time to be set apart! It was time for the Lord to be glorified in all my doings; and that He was. My husband even acknowledged, "there's something different about you." Yes it was. It was my New Man. His name wasn't Tom. It wasn't Dick, and it certainly wasn't Harry. His name was and is Jesus!

Jesus taught me how to love myself first, and He gave me a new love for this man who was unlovable. He taught me how to see past his flaws and look forward to His cause.

After I matured in this area, the Lord would have me stay home at times; or my husband would call and ask if he could come and see me; not just the children, but me. Sometimes, I made dinner, other times he would borrow my kitchen and cook for me. When I cooked, I would still prepare his plate and serve him, but it was the Jesus in me doing it. I would sit and sometimes talk with him or watch a movie with him, but it was the Jesus in me doing it.

My instruction came from the Lord. I did not understand the things He would have me do, but that grace…The grace of God will help us to endure impossible things, but there is always His expected end which we will all reach, if we just follow the One Who is all-knowing.

I did not know why He had me to buy a pedicure kit, but I know what I sensed the day I filled a basin with warm soapy water. I remember when I came down the stairs, spilling some on the carpet on the way down. I remember when I pushed the table forward to make room to sit at his feet. I remember when I placed his foot in my lap and gently removed one shoe and then the other; then one sock after the other and placed his feet in the warm water. My girls were there that day; watching me. This was ministry. This was the needful thing. This would be a lasting memory to them for life; not of me, but the God in me. This moment was a "yes you can" moment. In spite of all things, yes, you can represent the heart of Christ at all times. You can make it about Him even when it hurts. With every passing minute, with every stroke of the sponge; with every clipping of each toenail, the Jesus in me was loving the hidden man in him knowing that one day, he too would remember…but for now love would cover…

1 Peter 4:8

Above all things have intense and unfailing love for one another, for love covers a multitude of sins [forgives and disregards the offenses of others].

Chapter 3
Is Divorce Too Hard for God...

I am convinced that something miraculous happened in the realm of the spirit that night, but only time would tell. In the meantime I would have another test of faith.

It was March of 2007 when I came home to find a pink slip with a big black star on the front of it, taped to my dinner table. I was in utter disbelief. In that moment I felt as though God had actually forsaken me. After all I had done and allowed Him to do in me, I thought briefly that it had all been for nothing. I said to myself, and probably out loud...The devil still won after all that, God? I found myself questioning Him in my mind with thoughts like, "Am I just a fool, or am I being led by You? Would you leave me out here in the wilderness feeling foolish and ashamed?"

Wow! Then the thought came to mind, "but wasn't Joseph left for dead (at first)?" God had a purpose for all that Joseph would endure and there was an expected end. Surely, there was one for me, too, but for now...disbelief was my blanket.

Although my husband had told me he had really filed for divorce this time, a part of me did not want to believe it. I thought, even if it were true, surely it cannot amount to much because the Lord has shown me His plans. He has revealed to me that He is restoring my marriage therefore, it cannot possibly end. But the impossible was proving to be very possible even beyond the promise of the Lord. WHAT?

Oh my God, it is really happening! After eleven years, eleven months, twenty days and annual threats of divorce, it was actually time to face the fact that this was not just a threat, but a moment of cold hard truth!

Ouch! I remember my heart turning flips inside my chest. I did not know whether to be angry, cry, scream, pray or even simply be relieved. I also did not know if God was still with me at this point. As I ripped the pink slip off of my table and ran up the stairs to my bedroom I began to question immediately; God why have You forsaken me?

After pacing the floor in a state of bewilderment, I called a very close and trusted friend of mine and told her what I had found. Of course she counselled me and tried to lift my spirit but it was not happening, not then. I was numb! After that phone conversation I put the thought behind me just long enough to lie down. I tried to get a quick nap before I had to report to my second job.

Okay, no napping was going on here. My mind was racing in circles. How could this be? REALLY GOD???

I eventually got up and got ready for work. Life was happening around me and I remember it raining outside, but I was moving instinctively only. I had no life in me.

I attempted to work that night, but my focus was not on collecting money for missed payments on television entertainment. Actually, I had no focus. I was devastated! Thank God the storm caused our computer systems to go down at work and our workload was halted for most of the night. I was so grateful for this downtime. I needed to be able to seek some type of peace. Although, as the minutes ticked on, I found myself with more anxiety than I could contain. I felt as if I could literally crawl out of my own skin. I HAD TO LEAVE THIS PLACE! I COULD NOT STAND IT! I wanted to scream. I wanted to cry. I wanted to throw things. I wanted to talk to God face to face and ask Him why He had toyed with me all this time and caused me to build this trust in Him and this faith in Him to work miracles even in my life, yet He knew this day would come! Oh yea, I was angry, angry with God.

Finally, the night ended and I made my way to the parking lot. I sat in my van, not wanting to turn the key. After I did start it up I did not want to drive home. I willed myself to put it in gear and go on, but the tears came from out of nowhere. I believe the tears were streaming down my face faster than the car was moving from the parking spot, to the service road, to the back road which led to my townhouse. I started talking to God out loud as if He were sitting in the seat next to me. At first my tone was very low and almost muffled, but the intensity of my pain grew with each syllable until I found myself begging and pleading, then yelling and screaming at Him.

I had totally lost it! What was happening to me? I had completely checked out! This was a first for me. I had never been so out of control in my entire life. Was this the makings of a nervous breakdown? I was screaming at the top of my lungs. I was reminding Him of all the promises He had made and the dreams He had shown me. I told Him about the times I wanted to give up (and would have been justified in so doing), but how He would revisit me with another nugget of hope to keep me going. I told Him, "what about those who are watching; those who know I am believing You? What will they say of You if You do not keep Your promise to me?"

Then I remembered the words of my prophecy spoken in 2006 and reminded Him of that too.

God, YOU SAID… "the things you have been believing Me for are about to come to fruition and it will be like a domino effect. It's going to happen speedily, faster; it will not be long and drawn out…"

So, I said God, what did You mean when You said it would not be long and drawn out, cuz this, has taken a turn for the long, and I'm certain it will be drawn out! Lord, Your timing is not my timing. Your ways are higher than my ways and Your thoughts higher than my thoughts. Therefore, I need to know what You meant. What was Your timeline in all this?" I was still very passionate about getting answers from Him in that very moment and though I managed to drive home safely, I cannot tell you how I got there; but for His grace.

I went to my room that night distraught and confused but somehow, still hoping I would dream and that He would be there to meet me. I HAD TO HAVE ANOTHER DREAM!

When I awoke in the middle of the night I was frantically searching my memory for some trace of a dream, but instead reality phoned in that I had nothing more to hope for. The dream had not come, so there I lay in a state of utter devastation not wanting to lift my head from my pillow.

As daylight began to invade my darkness I realized I had gone the whole night without an answer from the Lord. I recall hearing knocks on my door from my children trying to get me to come out of my room that morning but I would not acknowledge them. I don't even remember answering them at all. I was utterly devastated still! I did manage to finally drift off to sleep one more time with one last breath of hope in my heart and wouldn't you know it, that's when I finally had the dream that changed my life for good...

In this dream I found myself in a church. I had walked into an intense time of warfare prayer. The ladies with perfect blue hair were fervently interceding as I took a seat on one of the benches. Immediately, the chief intercessor approached me and took my hand almost as if she had been expecting me. She looked very intently into my eyes and uttered this phrase, "I hear the Lord saying, three years for that for which you seek." OMG!!! Did The Almighty God just speak to me in plain English?

Now, reflect back with me as I remind you that I was neither respectful nor submissive as I called out to God. I had even threatened that I could no longer go on in this faith. While the Lord would have been justified if He had smote me dead in my tracks, He instead, was merciful. However, I cannot help remembering what the scriptures tell us about Uzzah in *2 Samuel, Chapter 6...*

6And when they came to Nachon's threshingfloor, Uzzah put forth his hand to the ark of God, and took hold of it; for the oxen shook it.

And the anger of the LORD was kindled against Uzzah; and God smote him there for his error; and there he died by the ark of God.

Uzzah was guilty of putting forth his hand to take hold of the ark of God. He simply put forth his hand. While this was a huge offense to the Lord, I would think that my behaviour would have superseded that act by leaps and bounds, but God in His infinite mercy not only spared my life, but He answered me in a most precious way. He gave me an absolute and tangible answer to my demands because that's just the way He is and that's just how He loves. For that I am more than grateful! I was overwhelmed with gratitude to say the least.

Three years? Three years? Okay, but what does this mean? Will we be divorced for three years? When did the three years start? Is that three years from now or three years from the time You said it wouldn't be long and drawn out? Okay, I didn't know exactly, but OMG, I just heard from God!

Although, I still had one concern; the pink slip...Thank You Jesus, but why am I here with this pink slip on my pillow where my husband used to be? This resembled neither restoration nor breakthrough.

I stayed there in my thoughts for several minutes. However, as I turned from that darkness to the new light of my dream I arose with new hope now that God is in control, so I placed the pink slip in a drawer without expectation that I would have need to face the accusations therein. I even entertained a few thoughts about how God was going to put the brakes on the enemy's plan to make permanent, the division between my husband and me. I could see him coming back and repenting while tearing the papers up. I considered that the Lord might cause some turbulence in the realm of the spirit and prevent this thing from happening, but there was something so strange and unfamiliar in all this. I asked the Lord, what is my expected end here?

Jeremiah 29:11

For I know the thoughts that I think toward you, saith the LORD, thoughts of peace, and not of evil, to give you an expected end.

I still believed in God's promises to me, but once again, how would He fulfil them? That was all I could think about. I remembered Joseph again, and all the hope I had once had and I reminded myself and God that He cannot lie! There had to be a reason for this too. I pulled the divorce papers out of the drawer and forced myself to read his accusations or attempts to justify the divorce. I found some of the things I read to be false but even if they had been one hundred percent factual, there was nothing in there which could justify a divorce according to the word of God, so I began to see that this was another spiritual battle and it was time to put my war clothes back on and go to war!

He stated that there were irreconcilable differences between us. What in the world are irreconcilable differences? All that means is somebody is not walking in grace; somebody is pushing to have his/her own way; somebody is refusing to forgive and somebody is puffed up in pride! Truth be told, there is no other explanation for irreconcilable differences, so there it was and it was called Pride! Well there is plenty of word to confess over that so now what's next? We no longer shared the same goals or friends. Okay, I could name at least ten people without even thinking or blinking, with whom we both had relationships. We just were not visiting them together anymore. We just were not having them over as much, but not because we had moved on, yet simply because we were living separate lives and there was a road block to unity. So, this would probably fall into the category of deception. So what do we do when we know what we are dealing with? We use spiritual weapons to pull down the stronghold!

2 Corinthians 10:3-5

³For though we walk in the flesh, we do not war after the flesh:

⁴(For the weapons of our warfare are not carnal, but mighty through God to the pulling down of strong holds;)

⁵Casting down imaginations, and every high thing that exalteth itself against the knowledge of God, and bringing into captivity every thought to the obedience of Christ.

Deception is a spirit (which I have divine authority over)! OMG! The Lord was giving me the battle plan. So, what's next? According to what I was reading we apparently had settled all of our joint debts but as I recalled, we still had at least five accounts which were in both of our names. So this too, was deceptive.

I began to see that there were a lot of things written in that docket which were simply untruths. Now, if I had just signed on the dotted line and agreed with those things just to give in and allow him to have what he wanted, I would have been just as guilty as any other for allowing this divorce to happen. Well, my conscience would not allow me to do it. My spiritual convictions would not allow me to do it and His grace within me began to soften me up and yet again reveal to me that this was yet another opportunity to grow in faith.

I deliberately located the paperwork revealing the joint debts we had just so I could be sure myself that this was not true and so that I could not be accused of manipulating this situation. To me, these were simply lies! I did not care that he had said these things, but if I would have to agree with them, it was not going to happen. I simply wanted to allow honesty to prevail.

But wait a minute... What is this...?

(I must have left the door open for doubt, because my thoughts changed almost immediately to, so what, if he wants his divorce I'll just give it to him. Who cares?) Just like that, all that tall talk and big faith and battle planning went right out the window and for exactly twenty-nine days, I did nothing in response to his accusations.

Instead, over the next several days I had a few pity parties and wallowed in fear and disbelief. I even tried to be mad at God, but He reminded me that I had stopped believing Him. I had grown weary and accepted the devil's plan over His. I questioned Him in my mind. What? Really, God? I believe I could imagine Him saying, "Uh, yes daughter, I Am still here waiting on you."

It had been exactly twenty-nine pitiful days, then, out of nowhere, I awoke with a cold hard dose of spiritual truth…*but they that wait upon the Lord shall renew their strength; They shall mount up with wings as eagles. They shall run, and not be weary; and they shall walk, and not faint! Isaiah 40:31*

Where DID that scripture come from? I hadn't read it recently, meditated on it or heard anyone say it. It just rose up out of my spirit. Wow! Thank you Jesus! Forgive me Lord!

On the morning of the thirtieth day, those words were stirring in my spirit when I arose. There was a new determination in me to fight. I did not want to win him, but I chose to fight the good fight of faith for the sake of God's glory; faith in what I knew the Lord had promised me and the reality of it not being over. I decided no devil in hell was just going to take something from me especially if he has to lie to get it! This was my husband and I would not just sign away my marriage or allow it to be put asunder based on half-truths.

I had to work that morning, so I got ready as usual and went in at my regular time. It was on this thirtieth day that I called an attorney to ask what would happen if I refused to sign the papers. I was advised that a divorce could still be granted eventually.

He asked if I wanted a divorce, what the accusations were, and if I agreed with them? I told him I definitely did not want a divorce, but would agree to it as long as the reasons were legitimate reasons and I could sign the papers without conviction. I told him that the accusations were not major but just not entirely true.

He advised that I could at least respond to them explaining that I contest the complaints and instead of a divorce being granted due to there being no response from me, a court date would be given so we could discuss the matter further before a judge. He asked what the date of record was on the letter and he was literally floored when I gave him the information. He all but told me it was too late, and that I should have acted sooner. He didn't say it, but I could feel him calling me an EXTREME idiot.

But, because I am a child of God, I believe he had no choice but to follow through by saying, "being that it's day thirty, the only thing you CAN DO is type your responses and hand carry them to the court house and file your responses today!" He told me, if the judge had already reviewed the file and found that I had not responded, the divorce may have already been granted, so I needed to act quickly just in case.

Okay, writing has never been a real problem for me, so I was confident that I could get it done. My only concern was that I was out of time, but favour really isn't fair is it?

Just like the story of Joseph, I can say "but God was with me"!

I had only brought the letter but I did not have the decree with me at work so the first thing was that I had to get home to retrieve it, but my schedule was full at work and it appeared that I would not be able to leave. I was stirring in my seat wondering what to do, but praise the Lord, the phone rang and it was my nine o'clock patient having car trouble and needing to reschedule. (Who is this King of Glory?)

Well, that would only give me an hour and that would not be enough time to get to my house and back, and so on, but I just about lost it when the phone rang a second time and the clerk at the front desk said, "Dee your ten o'clock just called and said he had gone to his private doctor and had the test there so he won't need to come." Say it with me…(WHO IS THIS KING OF GLORY?)

I could barely hold back the tears. I was so elated. I didn't have anyone scheduled for eleven, so now my entire morning was free. I went to my boss and asked permission to run a few errands and he allowed it without even pausing to think. Believe it or not I did not have a home computer at this time so I had to drive home to retrieve the divorce decree, bring it back to work, type up my responses to his allegations, proof it, sign it, copy it, and hurry down to the courthouse before my afternoon patients would begin to arrive. My heart must have been beating on the outside of my chest. But, when I got downtown with my paperwork and heard the clerk say, "no there does not appear to be a final docket here in your file, so I can place your responses here for the judge to review", I knew this was another small victory. Just for grins say with me again…(WHO IS THIS KING OF GLORY!?)

WOW! Only God could do such a thing. I had wasted twenty-nine of the thirty days to respond to this decree. What caused me to act on the thirtieth day? Why did the attorney give me that information? He could have just said it was too late. BUT GOD!

Once the reality of it all had set in, I was probably grinning from ear to ear. I took the liberty of playing different scenarios in my head of what was going to happen next. I was so proud to know the Lord. So, every day for a week, I expected my husband to come to me with a change of heart. I just knew that the Lord had stifled this devilish intrusion just to buy more time for him to (like the prodigal son) come to himself. I believed it even more so when I finally received a letter in my mailbox and yes, a court date had been set a whole six months away. Surely, it would not take God six more months to turn this around. I just knew that this was the turning point.

Of all the dates on the calendar, our court date was set for none other than September 11 of 2007. What? 9/11? A day that marked one of the most devastating events in the history of the United States was now set as the date for my marriage to end in divorce. I was almost proud of what I believed God was going to do. I thought, how dare you devil! You think you're going to end my marriage and you're going to do it on 9/11? Talk about a righteous indignation. I was almost puffed up. I was literally talking smack to the devil like, "No you didn't! I KNOW you didn't!"

Chapter 4
Surprised but on guard...

The moment I had been waiting for finally arrived. I remember getting a phone call from my husband and listening intently for some sign of change in his voice. It was even difficult to be patient at this point, so in the midst of the conversation, I told him that I had gotten a letter stating that we would be going to court in September.

Uh oh, what's this? It became apparent that he had no idea of this. What? My world was still. My anticipation was diffused by the reality of his disbelief. Oh no, this was not at all what I was expecting. As he hurried off the phone with me so he could call his attorney, I too was surprised. If referring to a game of chess, this was like the devil saying, CHECK!

Reality set in, and I saw that my husband had been so ready for the divorce to go through that he could probably taste it. I was a little deflated as I began to reflect on previous times when he had come around shortly after I had received the divorce papers. I believe I could see the pride in his face. He seemed to almost gloat even, Therefore, when I did not hear back from him after we hung up from the call, I assumed it was confirmed by his attorney that we would indeed be going to court and it would not be for another six months. I figured this to be the Lord's Check Mate, but why wasn't I feeling spiritually victorious?

Later that afternoon I had to go to his job (as I routinely did) to pick up our youngest daughter whose elementary school was just across the street from where he worked. I used to sit outside in the car and call him from my cell phone to let him know I was outside, (he never liked for me to come inside) but this day I had left my cell phone at home and I had to go inside. I was sure he saw me come in, but he did his best to avoid making any eye contact with me or even to say hello. When I tried speaking to him he barely mumbled a reply. I did not know why he was so angry with me (at first), but it did not take long to realize my assumption must have been correct and he had, in fact, gotten the news from his lawyer. So, obviously this was not the turning point I had been expecting.

It was disheartening to realize just how much he had been anticipating his freedom from me. I did not tarry in his workplace and did not hear from him for almost three weeks following, except when he would call to talk to the kids or if they asked to contact him. He seemed to be very upset at the sound of my voice even. I finally broke down and asked him what the problem was and he retorted, "I ain't got nothing to say to you!" Wow! After three weeks, he was still brooding. He did everything he could to resist contact with me and I finally asked again what I had done to upset him.

He told me I was just mean and he could not wait to be divorced from me. Ouch! That was a slap in the face. He even said I would do anything to keep him from being happy and going on with his life. He said, "Why would you want to be with a person who does not want you?"

Words like those used to make me cry, but I found myself smiling. Hmm... I did not acknowledge that statement as I understood it to be just another attempt to put me down. I told him I simply did not agree with the things he had said in the divorce decree and I had a right and even an obligation to respond to them. I could not agree with his statements and I would not sign off on it the way it was. I also reassured him that he could have his divorce but he would have to justify it with truth! He spouted off about some things, but I remember the Lord giving me peace right in that moment. I remember my tone changing and the gentle answers which turn away wrath began to spew out of me without any effort on my part. I understood that he did not want to be married to me, and I told him I have let go of you but God still has His hold on me and He is not finished with this. I did say however, I do not contest the divorce, but I do contest your reasons for it.

During the waiting phase prior to finding out our court date, I had been advised to seek counsel from an attorney just in case I needed one and I had done so. She had advised that if he and I could come to agreements on how those joint debts would be paid and how we would divide property and possessions, et cetera, he could still be granted his divorce without a need for a court appearance. All we would have to do is agree and make an addendum to the original decree. As I explained that to him, he seemed to soften a tiny bit as I could hear his tone begin to change.

Okay, so here it is...back where we started...we are actually getting divorced. But why am I still dreaming? What about my prophecies? Or would we divorce for three years and remarry?

As I lay on my bed one night and reminded the Lord what He said through His prophet, ("is there anything too hard for God? The answer is no! There is nothing too hard for God!" She said, "We bind the spirit of divorce in the name of Jesus!") I asked the Lord, "how can You tell me this and yet allow this? Father, what are You showing me?"

I went to bed that night and the Lord gave me yet another dream...

I was in the hospital with my husband, but I was watching him from a short distance away, almost in the corner of his room. He was lying there propped up on some pillows and he kept sliding down. He was so frustrated. The nurses kept coming in to prop him back up, but as quick as they could leave the room, he would slide right back down again. His body was rigid like a board. I finally went over to him and said "are you okay" and he said, "No, I can't hold myself up, my neck is stiff!"

Exodus 32:7-14

⁷The Lord said to Moses, Go down, for your people, whom you brought out of the land of Egypt, have corrupted themselves;

⁸They have turned aside quickly out of the way which I commanded them; they have made them a molten calf and have worshiped it and sacrificed to it, and said, These are your gods, O Israel, that brought you up out of the land of Egypt!

⁹And the Lord said to Moses, I have seen this people, and behold, it is a **STIFF-NECKED** people;

¹⁰Now therefore let Me alone, that My wrath may burn hot against them and that I may destroy them; but I will make of you a great nation.

¹¹But Moses besought the Lord his God, and said, Lord, why does Your wrath blaze hot against Your people, whom You have brought forth out of the land of Egypt with great power and a mighty hand?

¹²Why should the Egyptians say, For evil He brought them forth, to slay them in the mountains and consume them from the face of the earth?

Turn from Your fierce wrath, and change Your mind concerning this evil against Your people.

[13][Earnestly] remember Abraham, Isaac, and Israel, Your servants, to whom You swore by Your own self and said to them, I will multiply your seed as the stars of the heavens, and all this land that I have spoken of will I give to your seed, and they shall inherit it forever.

[14]Then the Lord turned from the evil which He had thought to do to His people.

Oh my God, can you say, "But the Lord was with me!" The Lord revealed to me that although He was orchestrating all necessary things to bring about change in my husband, his neck remained stiff. He was resisting the Lord. The Lord was answering my prayers but I believe my husband's spirit was so corrupted with his selfish desires that he was unwilling to yield at this point.

You know, there are times when we pray to God and ask Him to reveal things to us so that we know how to pray for the manifestation of His promise and God does reveal. He does His part even when we cannot see it. In those times we have often lost hope and begun to grow weary in our well-doing, but if we would only ask Him, He will reveal to us whatever we need to know in order for us to stay on guard.

What I saw in this dream was surprising to me, but it encouraged me to stay on guard. It was surprising because of the way the Lord was communicating with me. He is the Almighty God! He has no obligation to commune with me but He's so gracious that He met me in my time of need once again.

If you are no longer on guard; if you have left your post, I admonish you now to get back up and get back in the fight! Ask the Lord what is holding up your blessing. Do not ever lose heart and think that God has abandoned you or is simply not answering your prayers. Yes you are getting your prayers through, but there just might be a little resistance from the enemy. God showed me that my husband was stiff-necked or resistant to change. He did not say throw in the towel and stop believing Me, He simply defined for me what the stumbling block was to the next level of victory; a man who was stiff-necked. Okay, so what now?

Matthew 17:19-21

^{19}Then the disciples came to Jesus and asked privately, Why could we not drive it out?

^{20}He said to them, Because of the littleness of your faith [that is, your lack of firmly relying trust]. For truly I say to you, if you have faith that is living] like a grain of mustard seed, you can say to this mountain, Move from here to yonder place, and it will move; and nothing will be impossible to you.

^{21}But this kind does not go out except by prayer and fasting.

NOW LETS GO BACK TO WAR!

I had gone to bed weeping that night but Oh Joy! It certainly came in the morning. When I woke up from that dream, I had a smile on my face. I had a new outlook on faith and yet another divine perspective from God that He intended to do just what He said, but I would have to continue to remain steadfast and unmovable no matter what appeared to be happening in front of me.

I jumped out of that bed and praised God like I had lost my mind! I turned my praise music on and cut a rug like nobody's business. HALLELUJAH! LORD YOU'RE WORTHY! I was on guard once again.

Although we made the addendum to the original decree and I received the phone call from him reminding me of the set time to go to his lawyer's office to sign the papers, I was not let down when that day arrived. I was fasting that day! I was fasting for "this kind". All the way down to the lawyer's office, I still expected the miracle of a phone call or some other kind of intervention to keep me from going through with signing those papers, but all things (even going through with a divorce) work together for the good of those who love the Lord and are the called according to HIS purpose!

Romans 8:28

We are assured and know that (God being a partner in their labor) all things work together and are (fitting into a plan) for good to and for those who love God and are called according to (His) design and purpose.

As I spoke briefly with my pastor after it was done, I told him, "Sir, I really do not understand what is happening but I am at peace although this does not line up with the Lord's promise. He said He was saving my marriage, and I know He cannot lie, so I don't know why I am divorced; and in spite of it all, the Lord is still showing me things in my dreams." My pastor gently replied, "The Lord said He was saving your marriage but He did not say you would not divorce first." Whoa! Can you feel the power of God on that? He went on to say, "You don't know how the Lord is going to do it, but He will do just what He said. I am sure of it."

I knew he was right about that. I had the faith to believe it but at the same time I needed to hear it in just that way! It jolted me right back into my prayer stance and I began to search for the next possible avenue to breakthrough. What other stronghold was in the way? I prayed again that night... "Lord, he doesn't love me. He doesn't even know how to love me. How are you going to make him love me or even help him to grow in that area?"

I feel the tears flowing even as I write...I went to bed and there it was again...another dream.

In this dream I had come to visit a man at his home. I could see that he was very fond of me and his name was the same as my husband's. I went inside and he showed me into a nice living room or den area. I then realized that this was not just a man, but it was my husband, yet we were not married in the dream. After he escorted me to the room, he stepped out for a moment and a very meek and gentle woman came into the room. She sat on the couch with me and we began to converse. The only words I remember her saying to me were these: "He's going to tell you he loves you tomorrow."

Chapter 5
Tomorrow is More Than a Day Away...

Okay, now I don't know about you but in my mind, tomorrow means tomorrow. It means the day after today. It means when I wake up from this dream I can expect this man who just divorced me to tell me he loves me right? Well, when he called me and asked if he could come over I thought it was rather strange since we had just divorced, but I also thought, wow Lord You really are awesome!

He came over. He gave me a hug and kissed my cheek almost as if it was still his to kiss and he went straight to the couch to sit down. He asked me if he could watch the TV and I said okay. I called the girls to come downstairs and I went upstairs to my room. After a couple of hours he sent the girls upstairs and asked me to come down. I had been praying (for "this kind") but I did go. I was anticipating a miraculous moment, and could barely help myself as I gently sashayed down the stairs (knowing I wanted to sprint). However, he simply wanted to talk about how the Lord was blessing him in ministry and with some things he had been trying to do for some time. He explained some things about a street ministry he was involved in and made some other small talk before he thanked me for letting him come over. He stood to leave and I felt my heart drop as if it had split in two and equal portions of it were in each of my shoes. No, this can't be! God, You always do everything You say and this was supposed to be the day. But, nothing happened that day or even that week, so then, did I misinterpret the dream? Well, a thousand years is as one day and one day as a thousand years, so could it be that my tomorrow was not going to be a twenty-four hour turnaround? That's exactly what it meant.

How do I love Dee...

Over the next few months, (due to a burst of rage and a physical altercation) he would not visit the house at all. I would allow him to pick the girls up, but not to come inside. We barely saw each other or even spoke to each other. I just continued to pray and believe God. In the meantime I simply lived my life, worked my two jobs, took care of my home, my children and carried on as if I were not married (in the natural) but I did not entertain the idea of dating or seeking relationship with anyone because in my heart, I was married to my promise (that's the reason why I continue to refer to him as my husband). My promise from God was all I needed. It brought me peace which truly surpasses understanding.

I had been praying for some time now that the Lord would teach my husband how to love me. I felt that the greatest obstacle I would face in marriage to him would be that he loved me conditionally. I had to fit into a mould that he had fashioned in his mind for his perfect wife to fit into. This would not be possible for me or any other woman in existence, but this was a real factor in my life. My prayers to the Lord were specifically targeted for a divine intervention in this area alone.

As I am writing this, the Lord would have me to recall a time when I was desperately bitter in my heart due to the rejection I had experienced over many years, yet God would bless me with a love for a man who was anything but deserving (as I would define it). I did not love my husband based on emotions. I had none! I did not love my husband based on the way he made me feel. There was nothing to love about that. The intimacy we shared was not enough to sustain me, so there had to be a reason why I was able to set aside my personal requirements and love in spite of all these things.

I remember the day I was sitting in a church service and the guest minister was prophetically speaking about the power of agape love. He prophesied that God was supernaturally filling hearts with an ability to love with a God kind of love that hopes all things and endures all things, etcetera. It was in that same service that I caught a glimpse of my husband at my right hand side. I didn't even know he was there that day, but he appeared seemingly out of nowhere. In that moment I was overwhelmed with what seemed like a baptism of love for him. I remember how it descended upon me. I believe I felt it growing right inside my chest and I began sobbing uncontrollably as I asked God to take it away from me. No, actually I begged... "I DON'T WANT TO LOVE HIM GOD!" I literally went limp to the floor and with my face to the carpet I cried and prayed and pleaded with the Lord but it was a done deal. God gave me what I needed to complete the good work He had begun in me. As I would reflect on this from time to time, I realized that God really knew my heart's desire was to please Him. I had confessed this to Him time and again; therefore, He would grace me in strategic intervals with the things that I needed that He might be glorified in the end.

I prayed that the Lord would grace my husband with this same love. I interceded for him on a regular basis and truly believed that God would answer this prayer in due season.

Imagine my surprise when my husband asked one day, if he could come over and talk to me. He didn't ask to come visit with the girls, he asked to come over to talk with me. I was a little reluctant at first. This would be the first time he had been in my home in months. But we agreed upon a time and I awaited his arrival. The girls were already prepared for bed when he came and after he spent a few short minutes with them, he and I had time to talk.

He indicated he could feel that I had been praying for him because he just could not seem to stay away (I knew this was God!)

We talked a lot that night. There was a meekness on him that I had not seen in years. He finally asked if I still loved him and I gave him the same reply I always did. "The Lord has graced me with a love for you that I cannot explain." I told him yes I do love you.

He asked me why I still loved him. I never liked being asked that question by anyone, let alone him. My abrupt answer usually is simply, "BECAUSE I DO!" I don't need a reason. Agape love is unconditional. However, I shared the story with him about how God had moved in that church service and he seemed to be in awe of my explanation. But he said, with the utmost sincerity and compassion, "Dee, I don't love you like that."

My husband had told me for many years, "I don't love you. I will never love you. Nobody's ever going to love you!" Now I was sitting next to him hearing him say he didn't love me, but it carried no weight because there was no harm intended. He was simply telling me how he honestly felt. I remember feeling an overwhelming sense of peace. I did not feel threatened or belittled. I felt as though the grace of God was smiling through me. I told him that was okay (and it really was). He then said the one thing that caused me to know that God was the author of this script (so-to-speak). He said, "I want to love you, I just can't. I don't know how to love that way." Wow! (All we really need is a willing heart).

This was something I knew God could work with. At this moment, I knew there was just a short matter of time before the Lord would fulfil yet another promise; therefore, I told him if it was something that he really wanted all he had to do was ask the Lord to give him the grace to love me unconditionally.

It was in this moment that I fell in love with Jesus all over again. God is a promise keeping God to no end and He certainly hears the prayers of the righteous and answers them. My husband asked me in that moment to pray for him to receive agape love for me. WHAT? WHO IS THIS KING OF GLORY?

As many times as I had prayed for God to bless him with unconditional love for me I never once thought that I would have the opportunity to lay my hand on him and pray for him to receive it. Please do not underestimate the power of the Holy Spirit! Ask and ye shall receive! Seek and ye shall surely find! God is ever orchestrating and ordering our steps. The steps of the righteous are truly ordered by the Lord and if we would just hang in there with Him we would see the miracles, signs and wonders that follow them that believe.

God made a way out of no way. I thought this would happen by some supernatural means (not that this didn't qualify for supernatural) but I expected my husband to just show up at my house one day professing his love for me and then I would know that God had moved, but never once did I imagine I would sit beside him and pray the most compassionate and heartfelt prayer I had ever prayed. It was nothing forced. I did not pray down heaven or see any fireworks, but I did pray that God would honor his request and give him the desire of his heart.

After I prayed, it would appear that he was not moved by any of it. There were no tears. There was no compassionate exchange of words. Nothing! He just lifted his head and said thank you. He left quickly, almost as if he was running away. The spirit of discouragement attempted to sway my mind, but I had seen God move! Only God could have done this! Get thee behind me satan! WHO IS THIS KING OF GLORY? He's the One I know. The only One Who could make this so.

I had a new sense of peace at this point and I did not doubt that God was very much in control.

I would have a series of dreams after this night...

First I dreamed that I was very much pregnant and that I had gone in to the hospital for an ultrasound. As the technician captured images of the baby she called my attention to one in particular. It was not like an image but an actual full view of my baby's face. It was as if I was looking right at my husband's face. I even said to her, "I sure hope it's a boy because he looks just like his dad."

When I woke up from that dream it was confirmed in my spirit that this was God speaking to me.

Prophetically speaking, pregnancy indicates expectancy. What is also obvious to us women is the reality of what happens while you're pregnant. You know eventually you are going to give birth!

Why would the Lord show me that I was pregnant with my own husband? Now this may not make sense to the natural mind, and it shouldn't. But, when we desire to go deeper into spiritual things, the Lord begins to give us little nuggets of revelation to chew on. I take my dreams very seriously and I look for the Lord to speak to me in them. Therefore, I believe He did just that. I believe the Lord was revealing to me that this union between my husband and me was not finished. I was actually pregnant with him. He was mine to birth! Of course I don't mean that in the natural sense, but my labour would be to pray and intercede for his deliverance. I was to carry this burden to full term and not abort the mission that God gave to me. I would endure the aches and pains and labour for him until I birthed him into his destiny!

Remember, God will not put more on you than you can bear. Someone reading this or others with whom you share may arrive at the idea that I am a fool or that this is just too much for them to believe; and that is fine! I can understand that, but I can also understand that my faith walk is different than the average person's and just maybe because I'm willing to believe God for impossible things He does impossible things just because this vessel is yielded to Him for the using!

A short time after I had this dream my husband came over again and we talked about love once more. He seemed uncomfortable with the idea that I only loved him unconditionally, but that I had no feelings for him. I remember him saying that he didn't just want me to love him like that. He wanted me to have feelings for him. My reply to that was, "I would much rather love you unconditionally. Feelings can change like the wind. If I did not love you this way I would not still be here waiting for "the man" that God has shown me."

He wanted to be wanted and needed by me. I told him that would come "but for now this is where I need to be for God, for you and for me. This is best."

Again, he replied that he was not there yet, but he asked me not to give up on him. He said he wanted what God wanted he just didn't know if he could do it. What? The man who once said he would never love me was beginning to break. He wasn't there yet, but now he was asking me not to give up on him. I couldn't give up on him because I wasn't giving up on Jesus!

I pray that as you are reading these words you can see and hear the change taking place here. This was a man yielding his will to God, not the angry, unloving, selfish man who used to spit out insults without a second thought. This talk did not bother me. I understood that it was real to him and the Lord would grace me to be at peace until it was time.

Over the next several months we would spend a little more time together. On occasion we would go out to a movie or have a meal, but I resisted the temptation to get reattached to him emotionally. I never took our outings to mean anything more than two people out in the same place together. I was waiting for the Lord to reveal to me that I could open my heart up to receive from him, but until then I would remain on guard. I did enjoy his company and I started to like this new person that was growing right before my eyes.

It's a great thing for me that I remained on guard because my husband seemed to become very distant at times and we would go for a few weeks without much contact with each other. During these times I would pray and intercede but I would not try to call him and ask where he was or why he wasn't coming around. (Sometimes we just need to get out of God's way and allow Him to work.) Once we put our trust in Him, we don't need to help Him out. It is hard to grow weary when you are focused on the outcome of a situation instead of what it looks like in the natural. When

God shows you what He's doing, put on your seatbelt and go for the ride. You might pass up a lot of exit ramps and some cars may cut you off without so much as a signal, but the highway with Jesus will always lead you to the destination He has for you and trust me, He will take the shortest route. It is when we get in there and try to speed things up and when we curse those who get in our way and cut us off, or exit prematurely that we miss out on our blessing!

These times were strange to me but the Lord would strengthen me still with the little nuggets of hope as He continued to reveal things to me in my dreams.

I saw myself pregnant again during one of these dry spells when my husband's behaviour was somewhat confusing. In this dream I saw yet another ultrasound, but this time I could see my husband trying to stand up on the inside of me. He was like a toddler learning to walk but each time he would try to stand he would fall over and bump his head. After he did this several times, he appeared before me all grown up. As he stood in front of me I observed him as a movie camera pans a scene from bottom to top. I saw him from his feet to his head. He was young and thin like when we first met. He was beautiful. I was excited to see him there and I felt relieved that he was back to normal, but as I neared his chin there was something strange there. His face was partially distorted as if it were someone else's. From the side of his nose up to the left side of his head there was a mysterious personality that was not the man I knew.

As I reflect back on that I remember asking the Lord to reveal what this meant. It is one thing to suspect that a person has a split personality (as the world would call it). It is yet another when the Lord reveals (as I believe He did here) that there is still a stronghold here to deal with. God is so great that He allowed me to see something that I never could have seen otherwise. Now, my part in this was to war against the stronghold as the word of God admonishes in

2 Corinthians 10:4-5

4 (For the weapons of our warfare are not carnal, but mighty through God to the pulling down of strong holds;)

5 Casting down imaginations, and every high thing that exalteth itself against the knowledge of God, and bringing into captivity every thought to the obedience of Christ.

We have the power and authority to pray and war against anything that has exalted itself against the knowledge of God.

What I know about God is that He dwells in me and He says I have authority to trample serpents and scorpions and over all powers of the enemy so that nothing shall by any means hurt me! Whatever the stronghold operating in my husband, its intention was to do me harm. I could either sit back and take it or exercise my right to tear it down!

The strongholds of deception, confusion, separation, division, divorce, pride, fear, intimidation, disbelief, Jezebel, Delilah, Athalia and Leviathan all needed to come down. I didn't know which one or if I was dealing with all of them bound up together, but it was time to put my war clothes on and go in for the kill! Why else would God show this to me in my dream? Was I supposed to be confused or think, "Gee, that was a strange dream?" No! I had asked the Lord therefore I received help. I had sought the Lord, therefore I found that my husband was struggling to get free from something, but he was going to need my help and my faith and my obedience to God in order to get it! I am his help, mete for him! I am suitable for him and no other, therefore it was my task to take on. There was still some deliverance that needed to take place here. This work was incomplete and the bible reminds us still that "this kind goes not out but by prayer and fasting!"

Some things we have to pray and fast and war for! It was time again to go back to war!

I immediately called my pastor and told him what I believed the Lord was showing me by this dream. He prayed about it first then called me back with the counsel to seek God on a three day absolute fast. He encouraged me to pray first for the confirmation from the Lord that this was what I needed to do, but I tell you now, this was no doubt, a strategy straight from the throne room. I was ready for it!

I fasted and prayed for three days with no food or water! In that three days I had dreams of my husband and me going to a place called "The Cornerstone" for dinner. In case you don't know, Jesus is the Cornerstone! It was my husband's suggestion that we go here and when I asked (in the dream) why the Cornerstone, he replied, "It's the best place, right?"

I would have another dream of my husband and me going up some stairs to attend a wedding. This wedding was being officiated by a pastor friend of ours whose last name is "Golden". As we encountered him on the stairs, he and my husband were making eye contact with each other which seemed to indicate they were talking in code! I caught enough of it to know that he and my husband had arranged this time for our marriage without my knowledge. Finally, the pastor asked my husband about the rings, but he did not have any. At that same moment my best friend held out her hand and said, "You can use these." You should have seen my husband's face light up. The dream was so real I almost hated to wake up.

When I did wake up, I remember being excited that God was still keeping His promise and that it was just a matter of time before these dreams became reality.

Still some time past with its share of ups and downs but many more ups than downs. No matter what, my faith was extremely high at this point, but I still knew I could not get in God's way, so I continued to pursue my relationship with Him while I patiently waited for Him to finish the work He was doing in my husband.

Then it happened! One evening while I was talking to a friend on the telephone, I heard that distinctive call waiting sound. I looked at my phone, surprised that anyone would be calling me after nine o'clock. But even further to my surprise, it was actually after ten o'clock. I recognized the number right away…

CHAPTER 6

The Restoration

A very humbled voice was on the other line asking if I had a minute to listen to him. I explained that I was actually on another call. He immediately assumed it was one of my girlfriends and was let down abruptly when I said, "No, actually it's David" (not his real name). He asked if I wouldn't mind giving him a call when I finished my conversation. Now, bear in mind, my husband is not a late night person. I told him I would call but said it might not be right away. He insisted he would be awake.

I did not rush off the phone. As a matter of fact, I spent another thirty minutes or more talking to my friend but I did return his call. Surprisingly, he sounded very much alert. He said he was glad that I had returned his call and asked if he could just speak freely. He went on to say something like this… "I know you're not going to believe me and I guess I can't blame you, but I'm asking you to just hear everything I'm trying to say before you respond." He then said, "You're all I think about it. Whenever I do anything I think about you being with me. Whenever I go anywhere I think about you being there with me. I can see now all the things that I once had in you and I miss that. I know you won't believe this, but I do love you and if you will allow me the time again, I want to do everything I can to make up for all the things I put you through. I'm truly sorry. I repent to you and I ask you to forgive me." He said, "I know you've moved on with your life and you're probably seeing someone right now, and I don't want you to change that because of me, but I am asking for a chance to date you at least. I don't want to rush into anything. Where I have always messed up in the past, is that I have rushed back into our relationship knowing that my heart wasn't right but I would try to half-heartedly serve God. I always failed at that. I don't want to fail at anything this time. Can you consider the things I'm saying and pray about it and let me know what the Lord is speaking to you?"

Okay, as long as I had waited for this moment and as great as I felt knowing that we had arrived at this place in time, I now had a reservation in my spirit that cautioned me to not respond then except to say that I would pray. I also added that I did not want to date him.

I told him that he had more than enough time to know me. I had not changed and that he knew enough about me to decide whether he wanted to be with me or not. I said, I owe you nothing at this point. When you date someone, you're getting to know them. What more can you learn about me by dating me? I love the Lord and I follow Him. I am not perfect but I am a wife not a girlfriend. I told him that dating would be a setback for me simply because, it would cause me to put my life on hold for him to have yet another opportunity to reject me or turn me down and I was not going to go for that. Finally, I said, I do forgive you. I forgave you a long time ago, and I want the best for you, but when God promised me that He would restore my marriage, I don't believe He had this in mind. I told him to continue to pray and when he was sure of what he wanted he should let me know then. I was not angry. I was stern and a little disappointed.

One thing I know about myself is that I am a wife! I don't need a husband to make me a wife, I am a wife! I believe I was a wife long before I ever had a husband because the Lord prepared me to be one. I believe that is why the bible says, he who finds a wife finds a good thing. How can a man find a wife before he ever gets married if a woman doesn't' become a wife until she gets married?

It is not easy to be a wife. The responsibility that goes along with it, is not just being a bed mate or one who prepares the meals and takes care of children. A wife is mete (suitable) for her husband. She complements him well. She has the ability to calm him with just a word or a smile. She knows his flaws and covers him in prayer. She does not make him the hot topic in the break room at work. She knows what he's capable of in spite of what he might be doing and she speaks those words that edify him until she sees the change. She calls those things that be not as though they were. The heart of her husband safely trusts in her. It does not fear her wrath!

Being a wife is something I take pride in. I love being a helpmate to my husband. I enjoy praying for him and serving him as a wife should. I enjoy the ups and downs that marriages go through and watching God get the glory when we overcome and grow together through the trials. I want to love until it hurts. I want to believe the best for someone in spite of who I see and pray and watch it come to fruition. Anybody can throw in the towel and go find somebody else to relearn and be dissatisfied with. Or so what if you find somebody who you think is better than what you had. Maybe that's who you are, but because I know who I am and that God won't put more on me than I can bear, I choose to stay with Him and accept His grace! To be reduced to a girlfriend is not who I am or what I am called to be.

A girlfriend does not have the authority in the spirit realm to pray him through until he gets the victory. A girlfriend cannot put one demon to flight, let alone one thousand. When he's under attack and generational curses and covenants made with the enemy begin to manifest, what is a girlfriend going to do?

I've got too much in me to start playing around just to feel good for a little while. A covenant is a covenant and part of the problem in the world right now, is that we married, bible toting, tongue talking, Christians give up too easily. We trade in our spouses like our own personal happiness is all we were put on Earth to pursue. The bible says to seek peace and pursue it! We will minister to anybody going through anything and even encourage men/women to hang in there and pray but when it's our own man or woman needing our patience and understanding they get this…uh oh, I know he didn't! He don't know who he's messing with! I'm gone show him!

Show him what? That the Jesus in you is self-seeking (How's that possible)? He's on reserve for friends, distant family and co-workers or, maybe the pulpit, but not for the one you love at home. Excuse me but charity begins where?

At home! Maybe at home with your husband! It may begin with your son or daughter or anyone that fits in your situation but charity/love, according to *1 Corinthians 13:4-7;*

4 Love endures long and is patient and kind; love never is envious nor boils over with jealousy, is not boastful or vainglorious, does not display itself haughtily.

5 It is not conceited (arrogant and inflated with pride); it is not rude (unmannerly) and does not act unbecomingly. Love (God's love in us) does not insist on its own rights or its own way, for it is not self-seeking; it is not touchy or fretful or resentful; it takes no account of the evil done to it [it pays no attention to a suffered wrong].

6 It does not rejoice at injustice and unrighteousness, but rejoices when right and truth prevail.

7 Love bears up under anything and everything that comes, is ever ready to believe the best of every person, its hopes are fadeless under all circumstances, and it endures everything [without weakening].

Wow! Look at that! Those last two words are, "without weakening"!

Has your love or charity begun to weaken? Revisit this passage of scripture and ask for His grace. Somebody needs you right now. The devil is going in for the kill while you have aught against his prey.

I am not bigger or better than anyone, but if Jesus endured the cross for my sorry sake (having done nothing wrong to begin with), how can I not forgive someone who has wronged me or refuse to believe the best is yet to come?

Have you ever really messed up? How long did it take you to truly repent and turn that thing loose? Once you turned it loose, those who knew you when, probably had a problem with you for a minute as you began to prove to them that you really had changed. Let patience have her perfect work in you!

I knew by the grace of God that my husband would change. I asked Him first! Once He said it, I knew it would happen. So no, I'm no fool. I have never been one and will never be one except for Jesus! I just simply believe Him and I have the proof now that His way was the only way for me.

For a few more weeks, I watched for signs and I could see the time was drawing near. I could sense that the atmosphere around me had shifted. Something very new and very different was happening in the realm of the spirit and then…

I was at work one morning, sitting at my desk. I was writing out the next chapter of my first book in a notebook when there was a knock at the door…

I thought it was one of the Cardiologists who always knocks before he enters a room, but when no one came in, I said, "Yes?" The door slowly opened and there stood the makings of a broken man.

October 30th 2008

He was wearing a blue shirt with a black sports coat as he walked in with his head hanging low. I said, "Hey. What are you doing here?" Through a slightly shaky tone he muttered, "uh nothing much, I just thought I would stop by."

I said, "Okay?"

He asked what I was doing and I said, "Oh, just writing a chapter in my book. What's up?"

As he took a seat on the stool next to my desk, I looked up just as his bottom lip began to quiver and he began with, "I'm tired Dee. I'm tired!" Of course I asked what he was tired of, (while remaining poised and seemingly unmoved). On the inside I was saying "Is this You Lord?" "I'm tired of running…I just don't want to run anymore."

As difficult as it was for me to sit there without offering him my shoulder to cry on, that little voice in my spirit would not let me get up. I could hear the Lord saying he's breaking but he's not broken. So, I let him cry briefly before gently asking him what he planned to do.

He said he wanted to talk but not then; however, I did not think it was fair for him to come to my job and say he wanted to talk but then walk away without telling me what about, therefore, I probed. He would relent and begin to tell me how much he missed me. He said he really needed me.

Eventually I broke in and provoked a response to the "why me" question stirring on my insides. As he began to speak, I picked up a book that I had on my desk, turned to the blank page in back and began to jot down notes to recall later what he had said. I showed it to him as I did.

He commended me on some things he had observed or should I say some things the Lord had removed the blinders from, such as my spiritual growth, motherhood, and etcetera. He was proud of what he saw in our girls whenever he came by to visit. They could cook breakfast, lunch or dinner; and not from a bag or box but from scratch! The house was clean, etcetera. Then the focus shifted back to him. "Dee, I'm worn out. I'm tired of running and I'm willing to try. My heart is open." He asked could we just move slowly and not rush into anything but expressed that he missed my love and conversation more than anything. He said, "Dee, you love me. You really love me. No one has ever loved me like you do. People want things from you. They want to know how much money you have or what car you drive, but nobody really loves anybody for the right reasons. All you did was love me."

I asked, "What do you want me to say?" He said, "You don't have to say anything." After a long pause, he stated, "Can we just start with forgiveness?"

There was another long pause before he continued with, "Please forgive me for everything. I don't want to lose you. The thought of someone else having you bothers me. I just need to be able to start over."

Praise God! Hallelujah! All these things were sprinting through my mind but I was still cautioned in my spirit by the Lord's warning that he was breaking but not broken when he finally said, "I really want us to just go somewhere together." SCRREEEEEEEECH!!!! WHAT?

Okay, here's where I had to put the brakes on. Where could we go together? Now, I really did not know how the Lord was going to get us from this square to the finished line, but I did not picture us taking a vacation together for the fun of it either. Therefore, I could not resist saying that the only place we could go together would be a honeymoon. He quickly said, "That's okay too. But there has to be a process to getting back there. I'm ready for the process."

Now, in my mind, all that had happened since our divorce was "the process" so I wasn't entirely sure of what he was meaning. But just to be sure we were on the same page and that I had actually heard what I thought I did, I said, the only way we can go on a honeymoon is if we are married. He said, "I know. I know what you mean. Lets just not rush."

I said to him, "I'm not ready to jump back into a relationship right now. I want to seek the Lord for the right day and time and we will go from there." He said okay and added... "I don't know what's going to happen but I'm ready to try." WHO IS THIS KING OF GLORY?

Now keep in mind the Lord had cautioned that he was breaking but not broken so I was not going to jump the broom in the next twenty-four hours no matter what. I just knew that this was the breakthrough of a lifetime!

When he left my office that morning I was just down-right stupid! I know that's a little bit off the grammar path, but I wasn't good for anything the rest of that day. The Lord had literally blown my mind to bits and pieces! All this dreaming and praying and believing? All this craziness and strange behaviour and inconsistencies? All the tears and pacing the floor and pulling down strongholds! All the fasting ? All the many times I chose to show love in spite of the way I was feeling? Was this the reason why I did all that?

Over the next few weeks he began to come over to visit more frequently. We talked some things out. He answered a lot of questions I had about a lot of things that I still needed closure to. We had moments of laughter and fun and some moments of frustration and anxiety, but what I had more than anything was hope (no longer deferred) that the final stronghold; that face I had seen in one of my dreams, had been knocked out for the count and would not rise up again.

As we transitioned into the world of "whatever Your will is for us God," things were a little awkward at first. He had already begun to attend our church again although he sat on the opposite side from me, but he finally began to attend church *with* me. I was accustomed to sitting on or very near the front row and he began to sit next to me when he got there. Wish I could add the facial expressions of the congregation to this paragraph! Priceless!

We had long talks about what this was going to eventually lead to. I was not going to "date" him indefinitely but this would be a new courtship with God at the wheel. We began to pray together as the Lord paved the way for our new union.

There were daily signs that "breaking" was turning to "broken". Then it was confirmed! Almost as if it were on reserve for this point in time and he had reached up and pulled it out of the spirit realm, my husband began to tell me he loved me. As a matter of fact, he told me so often it was almost as if he wanted to get used to hearing himself say it. He told me he loved me daily, even more than once a day.

Yes, my "TOMORROW" had finally come. What I came to realize was that my tomorrow was not one, twenty-four hour turnaround but it was continuous. That is why he was telling me every day and several times a day. Every waking day was another tomorrow. All I had was my expectation for the next day, but His thoughts are higher! HALLELUJAH!

Things began to move quickly (or should I say, speedily/faster) just like the prophecy I shared earlier. Once he was able to tell me he loved me and mean it, everything shifted. He felt as though we needed counsel so we set up a meeting with our pastor to begin the process. The process was that the old covenant was severed and this would be a new thing. Everything then was then, but this would be a new union, forgetting those things which were behind and pressing forward toward the mark of the high calling of God through Christ Jesus.

It is almost as though we could not have gotten to this new place without totally severing the tie from the previous place. We had to divorce. When it was time to go forward again, there could not be any accusations like before, of trying to trap him by getting pregnant, or his feeling obligated to stay because of the kids, or that he had only married me for convenience etcetera. THE OLD EXCUSES DIED WITH THE DIVORCE! We had to put them in the ground and bury them. He would have to realize that he was without excuse at this point and that he was marrying me, not for convenience but because it was the will of God and the desire of his own heart.

After brief counsel with our pastor the only thing to do next was to set a date, which we did set for some time in January 2009, but that date would be postponed. Finally, he suggested another time frame but charged me with selecting the actual date. Although for the two weeks preceding the actual date, a spirit of fear gripped me and I bowed out. What? Yes, I was shaking in my devil-stomping boots!

I called my pastor and one of my best friends and explained that I could not go through with it. There seemed to be a disconnect or something seemed to be missing. Yes, it took me a minute to realize it was that power, love and sound mind that used to reside in the place that fear now occupied.

My friend of course, thought I had bumped my head. I will never forget her saying, "Now Dee, isn't this what the Lord said He was doing? I know you have not waited, prayed and believed all this time, to now tell God no!" My pastor pretty much shared her sentiment.

Ok, so what was I to do? The same thing I admonish you to do right now. I pulled out my journals and revisited all the dreams I had. I could recall each and every setback which the Lord backed up with a promise and one by one He had fulfilled them. I remembered the prophecy from 2006 and the dream He gave me to confirm that it would be three years until the manifestation. So then, why the fear? Did I really trust God? I would have to prove to myself that I did. How could I back down now?

Then once again, I saw your face...you, reading this book right now ...no longer holding that towel you once thought about throwing in. But holding on to your new found faith in our God Who keeps His promises even in this day and age. I thought about how many times I said, WHO IS THIS KING OF GLORY? And as I say with you, He is THE LORD STRONG AND MIGHTY. He is THE LORD MIGHTY IN BATTLE...I urge you to rejoice in your promise and embrace your dreams...as I did.

Troy and I had talked about rings and we had agreed that we did not want to remarry using the ones we had previously, but the timing was not right for us to go out and purchase new ones. But if you recall in previous chapters I revealed a few small details of a dream the Lord had given me which revealed where we would receive the blessing...

When my phone rang it was another close friend of mine. The lady calling was the one who had offered my kids and me a place to stay during my separation from my husband. She wanted to know if she and her husband could bless us by purchasing our new rings. (HOW GREAT IS OUR GOD!) This was exactly what the Lord had shown me. In the dream this same lady was the one who had held out her hand before my husband and me and said, "You can use these." In her hand were two wedding rings. Now here she was calling and making that offer to me. I was overwhelmed and vehemently in awe of God's faithfulness. I did accept as she asked me to choose the design but as she gave me the options, my only request was that she ask my husband to choose it for me.

I did not see the rings until the thirtieth day of May 2009...

CHAPTER 7
HE remembered me...

In my introduction I quoted Deuteronomy 31:6, which tells us that God will never leave nor forsake us. I know what it is like to feel left alone and forsaken, but notice that it is just that...a feeling. The enemy is sometimes very clever with causing us believers to feel something other than what God is saying or what He has promised. He has done this since he beguiled Eve in the Garden.

Eve allowed the enemy's words to overshadow the truth and caused great suffering, not just for herself, but for all women. Answer this for yourself, what is your truth? Is it what God said, or what the devil is saying? What effect will your decision have on your life or the lives of others?

When we do not keep our focus on Him and we allow the cares of this world to tempt our flesh, our spirit grows weak and we begin to believe God has abandoned us. The truth is however, God never abandons us. Usually we abandon Him. We grow weary in our well-doing and we give more credence to what we see over what we know. But He promised us that in due season we would reap if we do not faint.

Have you fainted? Have you stopped believing? Have you grown weary or thrown in the towel? I understand. I know how you feel and I remember the thoughts which can lead to despair, but again, I admonish you to trust Him. Walk by faith, knowing that His integrity is matchless! If He said it, He will do it. I have obtained that for which I so desperately hoped. Since He cannot lie, then surely you too, can take Him at His word and reap your reward. Remember, "Without faith it is impossible to please and be satisfactory to Him", so, yes, you have your work cut out for you but anything worth having is worth fighting for. But the battle is not and has never been yours; it is the Lord's, and He has never lost a battle!

I believe your God has picked a fight with the devil on your behalf and said, "What about my servant (your name)? I declare and decree that there is an enabling grace on you to endure UNTIL...

I pray that this story inspires you to do just that.

When I began to envision the domino effect of those who would stand, I said out loud to the Lord, "Lord, if You really do this, how many marriages will be restored?" I saw you in the possibility. I saw you woman of God. I saw you man of God, having done all, still standing therefore, with your loins girt about with TRUTH!

Search the word of God as I did and apply the truth of His word to every lie the enemy has whispered to you. What do you know about God? Write it down and ask yourself, what does His word say in spite of what you see? Write these things down and meditate on them. Be willing to let Him lead you and guide you all the way. Pay attention to your dreams. Write them down and meditate on them. Ask the Lord to interpret them for you.

Although, at times, I admit I got off course, I always picked back up and got back on track. You don't even have to get off course. Learn from my story. Glean from my mistakes and the times when I allowed the seeds of doubt to sprout up the fruit of despair. You don't have to do that, either. I am here to tell you, even if you are on the verge of divorce; there is NOTHING too hard for God. No, not even divorce is too hard for God. I have reached the other side of hope and we are still going strong. I know your pain and your frustration. I have been there! I can relate, but I pray right now that the peace of God which surpasses all understanding would overtake and overwhelm you even now in the name of Jesus! Together with you, I take into captivity every thought and imagination that exalts itself against the knowledge of God and say NO!

SAY IT WITH ME...NO DEVIL! God's got this! He made me a promise and I'm not going anywhere. I will see His promise fulfilled in me and in my life.

Will you endure to the end without fainting? Come on and say, yes, with me! What if things take a turn for the worse? Come on say with me, if God be for me...! Will you continue to profess His word? Don't you know, His word will not return to Him void! It will do exactly what He intends for it to do, in His timing. Will you continue no matter what? I admonish you to stand and Stand therefore!

Make it about Him. Imagine Him being glorified. That has brought a smile to my face and warmth to my heart many times over the years. I used to say, "I can because You did, God!" Amen!

I know you can too. I am praying for you!
COME UP HIGHER!

As I was escorted to the small room on the right-hand side of the church, I could not believe it was actually happening, but of course it was. Just as Joseph was given the keys to the city and authority over all of Egypt was given to him by Pharaoh, his promise fulfilled all those years ago, must have felt much like I was feeling at this moment. I wonder if Joseph thought, my God, He remembered me!

In that moment I felt fifty feet tall! I felt as though every tear had been worth it. I felt as though every prayer had been answered and every stronghold had been broken. All the weird, unexplainable things had worked together for the good of one who was "the called according to His purpose". Hope deferred does make a heart sick but for those who endure to the end, faith worketh miracles!

Faith is the substance of things hoped for and the evidence of things not seen. I hoped for my marriage against all odds and in spite of every obstacle. Now, the evidence of faith was here before me.

PICTURE THIS...

He wore chocolate brown pants and matching vest with a baby blue shirt and chocolate tie. My knee-length dress was cream with lace and satin trim. I wore chocolate brown and gold shoes with baby blue and chocolate accessories. The ceremony was short. All those in attendance were the prayer warriors who held me up when I would weaken and those real men, who are there for other men to lean on during their struggles; our beautiful girls witnessing the results of unwavering faith and our highly respected pastor of all pastors; with us through it all; speaking a blessing of restoration to shake heaven and earth.

NOW FAITH IS!

I got the revelation and the manifestation all at once. Now, right now, where I was standing, in that very moment in time, my faith was tangible! I could see it, hear it, smell it, touch it, and even taste it. I saw my husband standing with me and the great "cloud" of witnesses (our best friends) with us. I heard the sniffles, the whispers, the "thank you Jesus", and the loud stares of those in awe of Him. It was as if I could hear the silent gasps. I could smell many fragrances and aromas from people, colognes, perfume, food and sweet wedding cake. I felt the Lord touching my heart as I touched my husband's hands again, but for the first time. This new time was nothing like the old. I could taste and see that the Lord IS GOOD! No refreshments or wedding cake could mimic the sweetness.

My heart was pounding to the cadence of these words singing softly in my spirit...Who is this King of Glory? He is the Lord strong and mighty! Again I say, Who is this King of Glory? He is the Lord, mighty in battle!

His battle, if you give it to Him.
His battle if you listen to Him.
His battle if you follow His lead.
Your victory if you trust Him.

All the way to the end trust Him. How will you know when it is the end; when it is time for you to stop hoping beyond hope; or stop standing therefore? Not one second before everything He promised you is completely finished. Not one second before the manifestation of the promise He has made you. He cannot lie! He did not lie to me and He has not lied to you. Even if you have grown weary, I admonish you to get up and trust Him! He is no respecter of persons. What He did for me, He will do for you. Get back on the battle field. Recall everything that He said and confess it. Keep Him in remembrance of His word and believe UNTIL you receive. Hallelujah and Amen!

As I close this final chapter, it has been eight years since our reunion. God has blessed us both with a new level of responsibility for His Kingdom. We have both been ordained as pastors at our local church. We have purchased a new home and have now seen all four of our siblings through high school. My oldest daughter is very successful at her job which came by faith. My step-son is touring the world as a musician. Our middle daughter has graduated high school and is pursuing her heart's desire to become an actress while managing a retail store. Our youngest daughter who graduated this year has begun her faith journey in Christ.

The Lord blessed my husband to become partner in a new business for a short time before transitioning him into the political arena. In addition to that, we enjoy advising others who are beginning their union or needing strength to continue what God has already joined together. These are exciting times for us. We are still growing and still going...

One final testimony...

My husband leaves work each day at six p.m. My phone rings every day before six-thirty. It's always him. When he makes it home after his long commute, he walks in the house and his first question to the girls is, "Where's your mom?" He comes to find me wherever I am and each time I get three kisses. I don't even know when or why that started but now it's just fun. When he's away for an extra day, I get six...

As I am finishing this final page I am compelled to share with you a personal testimony. As I returned to bed this morning (it was two-thirty a.m., my usual prayer time), my husband was awake and smiling at me. But it didn't look like the same man I have seen all these years. This morning, I saw the man of my dreams, literally, the new one the Lord showed me all those times, who would truly love me. I was thinking in that moment, "Really Lord, is this him?" In that moment, my husband said these words:

"You are awesome Dee. You are so awesome! I am so blessed to be married to you."

HE remembered me...

Please feel free to message me or send prayer requests. I look forward to interceding for you and believing God with you for His promise to you. *Thank you for reading my story.*

I welcome your correspondence at Deeliveredandfree@live.com

Made in the USA
Columbia, SC
24 February 2024